# WHERE'S MY OTHER SOCK?

How to Get Organized and Drive Your
Parents and Teachers Crazy

Claudine G. Wirths & Mary Bowman-Kruhm
illustrations by Molly Coxe

Thomas Y. Crowell   New York

*Dedicated to our mothers,*
*Julia Thompson Gibson and*
*M. Evelyn Tracey Bowman,*
*our models as we've worked to*
*organize ourselves.*

C.G.W.

M.B.-K.

Where's My Other Sock?
*How to Get Organized and Drive Your Parents and Teachers Crazy*
Copyright © 1989 by Claudine Gibson Wirths and
Mary Bowman-Kruhm
All rights reserved. No part of this book may be
used or reproduced in any manner whatsoever without
written permission except in the case of brief quotations
embodied in critical articles and reviews. Printed in
the United States of America. For information address
Thomas Y. Crowell Junior Books, 10 East 53rd Street,
New York, N.Y. 10022.

Library of Congress Cataloging-in-Publication Data
Wirths, Claudine G.
  Where's my other sock? : how to get organized and drive your
parents and teachers crazy / by Claudine G. Wirths and Mary Bowman
-Kruhm.
     p.    cm.
  Summary: A self-help manual for students, offering practical
suggestions for becoming better organized.
  ISBN 0-690-04665-0 : $     . — ISBN 0-690-04667-7 (lib. bdg.) : $
  1. Teenagers—United States—Life skills guides.   [1. Life
skills.]   I. Bowman-Kruhm, Mary.   II. Title.
HQ796.W53   1989                                          88-39338
305.2'35—dc19                                               CIP

1   2   3   4   5   6   7   8   9   10
First Edition

# CONTENTS

Introduction    v

Getting Started    1

Finding *Your* Way    12

Making School Work    25

Planning to Study    37

Taking Your Time    51

Troubleshooting    63

Finishing Touches    72

Appendix    84

# INTRODUCTION

WHEN are you going to clean your room?

WHERE is your homework?

WHY are you late for school again?

Do you ever hear questions like these? If so, this is the book for you!

We wrote this book for you if you kick stuff under your bed. Or if you sometimes forget homework. Or if you're late a lot of times.

Maybe you think getting organized is too much trouble. Or maybe you even like being a little messy. Or maybe you don't know how to get yourself organized.

But we bet you don't like people nagging you about being messy, or careless, or late. In this book we'll tell you our secrets for getting organized, and we'll show you some tricks to organize yourself, your stuff, and your time. We can't promise these tricks will make you perfect. We *can* promise they'll make life easier for you.

These tricks can do something else for you besides cutting out a lot of nagging that you get. They can give you *personal power.* Think how you feel when someone fusses at you to clean up your mess. If you feel helpless and angry when that happens, you can feel powerful by using these tricks. You won't have to ask your mom (or dad or whomever), "Where's my other sock?" When you are in control of yourself and your stuff, you'll know where your socks are and you won't get *that look* when someone hands you a stray one.

In fact, if you learn how to use the secrets in this book, your family and your teachers will go crazy trying to keep their stuff as neat as yours! The truth is that lots of grown-ups don't know these tricks. That's why people often tell you to get organized, but they don't tell you *how* to do it!

Give this book a try. If it doesn't help, you can always go back to doing things the way you did before. What do you have to lose?

# GETTING STARTED

Aw mom, do I hafta? I'm already late for school.

Tell us about yourself. What do you think is the hardest part of getting organized?

**Big problems—like getting my stuff ready for school in the morning. I do okay with small things.**
Well, we've got good news for you. You'll never have to handle a big problem again!

**Sounds great! What's the catch?**
After you learn our secrets, you'll have to decide if there's

a catch. We know three secrets that will help you get better organized than you ever thought possible.

**I'm not sure I want to be more organized. What would my friends say if I suddenly started getting all dressed up? They'd think I was showing off or something.**

Being organized doesn't mean you get all dressed up. You'll keep on wearing the same clothes, acting the same way. You don't have to make a big thing about it and act stuck-up or better than anybody. The main difference is that you'll be more in control of your life. Even better, people will quit nagging you as much.

**That I'd like. What would I have to do?**

For starters, you need to know the three secrets. Here's the first one.

SECRET #1. *Break all big problems into little ones. Little problems are easier to solve.*

**How do I do that?**

Suppose you have a big problem—like getting to school on time. Picture yourself all snuggled down under the covers sound asleep. In this book we'll use the word *mom* to mean your mom, your dad, your grandparent, your housekeeper, or whoever takes care of you. Whoever that person is, we bet it goes something like this:

*Mom: Time to get up.*
*You: Mumph.*

*Mom: I mean it. The dog needs to go out. You don't want to be late again.*

*You: I'm up. I'm up. I just can't find my shoes.*

*Mom: Look in the bathroom. I saw them there last night. Now hurry up. If you don't get in the kitchen soon, you won't get any breakfast. And you're not eating until that dog goes out.*

*You: Can't you take him out? I can't find my homework. My teacher will kill me.*

*Mom: When are you going to get yourself together?*

**For sure—that's me!**

Being late for school is the big problem. Instead of trying to solve it, work on the little problems that slow you down in the morning. What are some of the main ones?

**Probably finding my clothes and books and stuff when I'm sleepy. Also, I hate hearing Mom tell me again and again to get up, so I don't get up when she calls.**

Solving the second problem is easy. *You* get yourself up in the mornings. You don't need your mom to do that. Buy your own alarm clock. There are all kinds of new ones in stores today. There's one shaped like a baseball that you throw on the floor to turn off! There's another one that you set to tell you a recorded message. Besides the crazy ones, there are clock radios and wind-up clocks and digital watches. Be sure to get one loud enough for you to hear.

From now on, let the world know that *you* will get yourself up on time. This won't keep you from being sleepy when the buzzer goes off or the message sounds. But you won't start the day staying in bed because you feel your mom is picking on you. You'll get up and get going because *you* choose to.

**I could do that. But what about my clothes and books? Mom says I should get them together the night before. And I don't get around to stuff like that. Takes too long.**

How long does it take?

**Gee, I don't know. I never timed myself.**

We bet it doesn't take as long as you think it does. We bet you can get everything done in about ten minutes. How about organizing your things in the evening during TV commercials? Commercials are about two minutes long and you have at least four or five commercials every hour—so that's almost ten minutes every show. What do you think?

**Well, during one commercial I could find my homework and books and put them by the front door. Then in the morning I could grab them on my way out.**

That's the idea. If you can't put them by the front door, put them by your closet. Or put them on top of the bedroom chest, where you'll see them when you dress.

During another commercial, check out the clothes you want to wear and be sure they're not in the wash. If you want to be really clever, hang all the clothes you are going to wear on the same hanger in your closet. Put your shoes right under them.

**That sounds okay. Anything else I could do during commercials?**

You could stuff your socks in one shoe so that you won't have to look for them. While you're at it, put a pencil and a pen in the other shoe. That way you'll be sure to take them to school.

4

**That's a lot to do every night.**

Not really. If you have trouble keeping it all in mind, jot down on a card the things you do at night to get ready for school. Tape the card on your mirror. Check that card each night before you go to bed. In a week, you won't need the card anymore. You'll remember what you need to do because you'll be in the habit.

**That might work. But here's a tougher problem. I like to take my own lunch on days I know the cafeteria is serving "mystery meat." But I can never find time to fix a lunch in the morning.**

How about making sandwiches at night while you're eating your last snack? Refrigerate them in a bag with some fruit. If you have a freezer, you can make a batch of sandwiches Sunday night for the whole week. Take one out as you need it.

**I begin to get the idea. What do I do about remembering money for school or my key?**

Pick a special place and always keep your money in that place. Do the same thing with your key. If your folks will let you, put a key hook on the wall near the door. Keep your key there all the time. If you hang the key on the hook as soon as you come in, you can grab it on the way out. Some people like to use a brightly colored key ring or cord so that it is easier to remember.

**Okay. But how can I remember stuff that I don't take to school every day—like a library book or a special report?**

Try a beeper. Doctors and other people use beepers that buzz them for something important. Your beeper won't be electronic, and it won't sound a loud "BEEP!" that everyone can hear. Yours can be a button, a bolt, a marble, or any small thing. It just has to be something out of the ordinary. Keep a box of beepers on your desk or dresser. Food isn't a good beeper. You might eat it and forget what you're trying to remember!

When you *must* remember something in the morning, put one of the beepers anywhere that you are sure to find it when you are getting ready. You might put it in your shoe or, in the winter, in your gloves. When you see or feel the beeper, your brain will go "BEEEEP!" to let you know you have forgotten something important.

**That's not a bad idea. Could I use beepers in school, too?**

Sure, and since you choose what your beeper will be, nobody but you knows when you use it.

**Hey, I can think of lots of ways I can use beepers.**

Hold on! If you get used to seeing them, your brain won't "BEEP!" anymore. Use beepers only for certain things that you *have* to remember—something special that you don't do every day.

**My sister writes notes to herself. Does that work the same way?**

It does if she remembers to look at the notes. If you like the idea of writing notes, try using those little colored pads that are sticky on the back, and stick them on your books or backpack.

**I've thought of getting a backpack. The other morning I ran out the door, tripped over nothing, and dropped my books. When I leaned over to pick them up, my money fell out of my pocket.**

The nice part about a backpack is that you can put everything but your lunch in it the night before. Then you can grab everything you'll need in one swipe in the morning. (Even when you're in a hurry, put loose papers in your notebook—not your backpack. If you just stuff them in your backpack, it'll be June before September's science homework comes to the top. See Chapter 3 for notebook ideas.)

Mark your backpack inside the cover with your name and phone number. Don't put your name and phone number outside. That's private information.

**Some days even a large backpack couldn't hold everything I need.**

On days your backpack won't hold everything, put your lunch, your notebook, and anything that might break in the pack. Carry in your arms only books and things that won't fall apart if they drop.

Some people like to carry the extra stuff in one of those neat canvas tote bags. When you go on vacation, you might buy a special one that you can use year-round. Others prefer to use duffel bags. Use anything that will help you keep your school stuff together so that you can move it quickly and easily.

**As long as I'm getting everything done the night before, I wish I could make my bed at night, too. I hate making my bed. Why do people make beds, anyway? They just mess them up again.**

People have very different ideas about how neat a house should be. Since you'll live in your folks' house until you grow up, you have to go along with what they like. Someday when you have a place of your own, you can keep it the way you want.

But if you don't make your bed, you're going to find that you lose things like pencils and clips and the dog down in the covers.

**Until I get my own place, how can I make my bed in a hurry?**

There are a couple of different ways to solve that problem.

Try a duvet (doo-vay). That's a washable cover over a comforter. The cover is made of two sheets stitched together on three sides, with snaps or a zipper on the fourth side. Stuff your comforter inside and snap or zip it up. Since you don't use a top sheet, spread the duvet over the bed when you get up and you're done. It takes only a few seconds. You can buy a duvet, or if you are handy with a sewing machine, you can make a cover to go over a comforter.

If you don't want to use a duvet, how about a sleeping bag? They come in lots of different colors, designs, and weights. Use a sheet insert. If you can't buy one, fold a sheet in half the long way and stitch the bottom and side. Whether duvet or sleeping bag, just smooth your covers and be on your way.

On the days you run late, at least close the door to your bedroom so that no one else has to see the mess!

**There's another reason I'm late some mornings. Sometimes I stay up late and watch TV. I get started watching a show, and before I know it, it's an hour later. And there's always another show after that.**

There are some facts of life you just can't get around. If you don't get enough sleep, you're going to be sleepy. If too much TV is a problem, you will have to plan your TV time. On school nights, plan to hit the "off" button at the very end of the last show you can watch and still get up on time. Don't be suckered in by the ads for the next show. Don't let the TV tell you what to do. Save late-night TV for holidays and weekends.

**But sometimes there's a show I just gotta watch.**

If you have a VCR, tape it. If not, ask a friend to tape it so that you can watch it at their house on the weekend. Don't forget, most really good shows are repeated in the summer. If you miss one, keep an eye out for its rerun.

**Even on nights I don't watch TV, I don't go to sleep when I should. I usually stay up until somebody tells me to turn out the light.**

Then you need the next secret to getting organized.

SECRET #2. *Be in charge of what you do. You CAN take control when you really want to be in charge of your life.*

**What does that mean?**

Just what it says. It means you *can* turn the light out and go to bed when you think you should.

Prove it to yourself. Tell yourself to count to ten. Then do it.

**That's easy. "One, two, three, four, five, six, seven, eight, nine, ten."**

Count to ten like that whenever you think you can't make yourself do something. That will remind you that you can be in control. Then reach for the TV "off" button, or turn out the light, or do whatever else it is you need to do.

You have real power. You know what you need to do to feel good about yourself and your life. Do it.

**I see what you mean. If I want to get to school on time, all I have to do is make changes in the little things I do the night before and in the morning. I turn my big problem into small ones.**

Right! Are you ready for the next step in getting organized?

**I guess so. Getting organized isn't as hard as I thought it would be. So far, I don't see anything I can't handle. So what's the third secret?**

Read on to find out.

# FINDING *YOUR WAY*

Do you remember the first two secrets? Since little problems are easier to solve than one big one, we told you to *break all big problems into little ones.* Then, because we know that you can make some good decisions that will help you organize yourself, we told you to *be in charge of what you do.* Now we'll tell you the third secret. It may be the most important one.

SECRET #3. *Find a way of organizing that is right for you. No two people organize exactly the same way.*

**Are you saying I need to do things my own way?**

Yes. You'll find that some ways of organizing will work better for you than others. What works for your mom or best friend may not work for you.

**Try and tell my mom that.**

If you show your mom you know how to organize your stuff, you won't have to tell her anything. Except maybe how you do it! Most grown-ups don't care how you organize—just as long as you do it. The important thing for you to do is to find your best way.

**How do I find my best way?**

Whenever you face a big organizing problem, pretend you are from outer space and you are seeing the problem for the first time. Think about different ways you might solve the problem.

**Do you mean that every time I organize something I will have to try two or three different ways? Forget it! That's too much work.**

Don't panic. We're trying to save you work. Don't get hung up on one way of doing things. Try one way, and if it doesn't work, try something else.

**How could I use this secret to organize the stuff in my room?**

First use Secret #1 and break the problem down into smaller ones.

To start with, decide if you are a "keeper" or a "tosser." The world seems to be divided into keepers and tossers. In a family where everyone is a keeper, attics and basements are usually filled to the brim with bags and boxes. In a family of tossers, the house may look positively empty to a keeper!

### Isn't organizing easier for a tosser?

Only because they have less stuff to deal with. How much stuff you keep isn't as important as what you do with it. Tossers who aren't organized may have more work to do than a keeper, because they throw away things that should be kept. For example, they may have to rewrite an English theme because they threw away the outline too soon.

### I save all my junk, so I guess I'm a keeper.

Since you are a keeper, plan on using *lots* of boxes and bags or shelves!

Next (whether you are a keeper or a tosser), decide if you are happier with things where you can see them, or if you like things out of sight. If you like things where you can see them, use shelves. If you like things out of sight, use storage boxes and bags. (See the Appendix of this book to tell you how to make more shelves and storage boxes for your room.)

**Okay. I'm a keeper and I like things where I can see them. Now what?**

Now that *you* have decided that *you* like keeping stuff and want it where you can see it, decide how *you* want to store it.

Here's a plan that works for many people. They put stuff they use every day close at hand, either out front or near the top of where they use them. For example, put pencils and pens on top of your writing place, your comb under the mirror, and the dog leash on a hook by the back door. This is where you need to decide what will work best for you.

**Then what?**

Decide which stuff is most important to keep safe. (Social security card? Medals? Pictures?) Put the important things in some safe place where they won't get lost, damaged, broken, or used every day. Don't forget where that place is. Write it down somewhere—maybe in a diary—so you can find the things again if you don't use them for several months.

Put things you need everyday somewhere where you won't have to scramble through a bunch of stuff to get to them.

**I've got a lot of little stuff that I don't know what to do with.**

To get rid of all the little stuff, try a corkboard in your room. It will hold all those pictures, ticket stubs, free coupons, key rings, etc., that usually end up in your way on top of the dresser or desk. (Buy a big sack of pushpins and keep them handy, so when a new picture comes in, you can pin it right up.) Fill a large can on your dresser with anything that won't hang up.

**I haven't got space on my walls to put a corkboard, but could I hang a sheet from the end of my bed and stick stuff on it with pins or tape?**

That sounds like a neat idea. Now you're using Secret #3. You are doing things your own way. Just to be safe, check with your mom before you hang anything up in your room. She may want you to use special tape or pins.

**Okay, but my walls aren't the only places that are crowded around here. I need to throw some of the stuff out of my room, but where do I start?**

Only you can decide what you want to throw out, but here are our ideas.

First, look hard at everything in your room. Ask yourself if there is some furniture in your room that you don't use. Could it be moved somewhere else in the house?

Ask yourself if there are some things you can throw away because they can't be fixed or you don't need them anymore. Check out old toys, little-kid books, a broken skateboard. (Be sure a parent checks before you get rid of anything that might be valuable. They might think something is worth keeping even if you don't.)

Ask yourself if your hobbies and interests have changed. Can you give some things away? Some younger child might like part or all of your collection. They also might like a neat jacket that you don't wear anymore.

**Mom already gave away some clothes I've outgrown, but**

**I still don't have enough room in my closet. I have winter and summer stuff all smashed in there together.**

The second step in getting more space is to look at how you store things. Store off-season clothes in big plastic trash bags. If your house has a storage area to keep the bags, great. If not, stick them in one end of your closet. The clothes will still take up less space than if they're loose in drawers or on hangers.

Have one bag for clothes that you wear only in the very hottest part of summer or the very coldest part of winter. Don't mix a jacket that you may want on a cool fall or spring day with your bathing suit. You'll be angry when the weather changes suddenly and you have to dig to find it.

Be sure, of course, that all the clothes are clean and dry, or they will mildew and wreck everything in the bag. Tie the bags shut and stick on a piece of tape that says what's inside. Believe us—you won't remember what's in a certain bag later even though now you are sure you will. Let your folks know what you are doing so that they won't think the bag is trash and throw it away.

**My closet shelves are also a mess. I can't reach things on them very well either.**

Don't just pile sweaters and things in the closet. Put them on the shelves in cardboard boxes. You can decorate the boxes with pictures of what's in them. Boxes are easier to handle than loose clothes.

To get more hanging room, buy a small, short rod you can hang from the higher rod. That gives you room on both rods for short things. You can even make a small rod yourself from an old broom handle. Ask your woodshop teacher how to do it safely.

**I've always put socks and underwear in the top drawers of my dresser and the rest of my clothes in the bottom drawer. What do you think of that?**

That's probably the way most people do it. Again, whatever way seems right for you is best. You could, for example, put your clothes in the drawers by outfits. Roll a pair of socks, some underwear and a top in each pair of jeans. Or you could put clothes in the drawers by the order in which you put them on—underwear and socks in the bottom drawer, jeans in the middle, and tops in the top.

If you have trouble remembering where things go, ask your mom if it's okay to put a label or a sticker on the drawers.

**Mom is always fussing about the junk under my bed. What can I do about that?**

There's nothing wrong with *storing* things neatly under your bed. You can buy special under-bed cardboard storage boxes for only a couple of dollars when they go on sale. They look neat, keep things clean, and are easy to move when you vacuum under the bed.

It's probably the cola cans and the sweatshirt that you kicked under the bed that she minds. Sounds like you need to get a larger trash can for your room and to make a quick trip to the clothes hamper.

**Someone's always in the bathroom where the hamper is.**

Why not put another hamper in your room? If you're really

short of space, use a laundry bag. Hang it on a hanger or the back of a chair. It takes up very little space and is easier to carry to the washing machine than most hampers. Make your own out of a king-size pillow case and a coat hanger. Then use it. Old underwear under the bed doesn't die, and it doesn't fade away either!

**A hamper in my room might help with keeping my socks together, too. When I get ready to put on my socks, I usually can't find two alike.**

Sometimes it seems as if a sock-eating elf lives in the washing machine. One of the easiest ways to keep a sock with its mate is to hook them together when you take them off. You can buy a cheap pack of special plastic rings made for that. Just slip the toes of both socks through a ring. Toss the socks in the wash and pull off the ring when you're ready to put them on. Keep a dish or box of the rings on your dresser.

Buying socks in white or only one color is another way to save time you'd spend looking for sock mates.

If you can't tell your socks from those of everyone else, use a marker pen that won't wash off to put your initial on the toe of each of your socks.

**I've got one of those pens. But it's buried underneath all my books and papers. I don't have a very big desk, and I'm not always sure what school papers I should keep and what I should throw away.**

That's a tough problem. Deciding what to keep isn't easy.

You should have a box of school papers that you keep forever (or at least until you're grown). In the keep-forever box, put your old report cards (no matter how bad!) and any papers from school about requirements or special honors or special punishments. You might need them when you go job hunting someday. Even if you don't, they'll be fun to look at ten years from now.

You'll also need an everyday box that you keep just for the present school term and clean out at the end of the year.

### What goes in that?

Throw in all official school papers like absence slips or receipts for money you paid for field trips, gym towels, etc. Also keep this year's old homework and tests—especially old tests. Keep them in folders by subject. Why tests? Use them to study for finals. They remind you what kinds of questions each teacher asks and what each teacher thinks is important. It's smart to study with the teacher's questions in mind.

Most other things can be thrown away.

### I can't bear to throw out that science paper I got an A on last week.

Of course not. By all means, keep some special papers and things that you want to remember in a "memory" box. You're the only one who knows what to keep in that box. Just try not to keep too much.

### You know, when I get all that stuff out of my room, it should be easier to keep clean. I wish there was some magic way of cleaning my room.

There's no magic way, but there is *your* way. Secret #3 to the rescue!

**There's more than one way to clean my room?**

Sure. Look at cleaning your room as a big problem. Secret #1 says to break it into little steps that are easy to do. The steps in cleaning a room might be: (1) Get started. (2) Choose a way to sort your stuff. (3) Put things away. (4) Dust and vacuum the room.

**But how do I get started?**

Decide whether (a) to pick up stuff *in* the room as you clean or (b) to pile all your stuff out in the hall and put things *back* into the room after you clean. Some people like the second way because they find it easier to know where to put things in a clean room.

**Then what?**

Then choose how you want to do steps two and three. (Choose one of these ways or make up your own.)

a. Pick up things one at a time and put them where they belong, or—

b. Pick up and put away all of one kind of thing. For example, first pick up all clothes and put them away. Then all shoes, then all tapes, etc. A similar way is to pick up all red things, then blue things, and so on, or—

c. Pick up all things that go in the closet and put them in the closet. Then the things that belong in the chest, then in the desk, then in the bookcase, and so on.

**I sort of like starting by taking everything out of the room. But wouldn't putting it all back take a lot of time?**

You bet. But other ways do, too. Whenever you plan to tackle a big problem—like cleaning your room—set aside enough time to finish the job. Once you start, dig in until you are through. If you get almost through and then stop "just for a little while," you almost never finish the job. Then you feel guilty and frustrated.

**But I get bored working a long time by myself.**

Then find a way to keep from being bored. Some people can work with a friend. Ask a friend to help you. Offer to help clean their room next week.

If you can't work with a friend, dig out an old tape you haven't played in a while and play it while you work. You might even listen to a good mystery book on tape. Most libraries lend all kinds of taped books for free.

Make organizing a game, and you make the rules. To make it a real game, ask your mom to hide a dollar bill somewhere in a seriously messy room! You get to keep the dollar if you find it and you finish cleaning your room in less than two hours.

**When my room gets in a big mess, I get so discouraged. I can't even remember what it looked like when it was clean.**

Try this. The next time you get your room just the way you want it, take pictures of your clean, neat room. Put those pictures on your mirror or your bulletin board.

Next time your room gets messy, the pictures will prove that you can do the job. They'll also remind you where things belong and will help you organize more quickly.

**That's a neat idea. Maybe some weekend when I have to**

clean my room, I could call a couple of my friends who have to clean their rooms. We could photograph our rooms before cleanup and then after. One of our other friends could judge the photos to see who had the hardest job!

Great! Maybe you could also treat yourselves to lunch after the great cleanup.

**I can tell you who will be the loser in the photo contest. The kid who lives next door to me is a Super Slob. He never gets his room clean.**

Let's face it, all of us are Super Slobs in some part of our lives. But most people have an Organized self as well as a Super Slob self. We bet your friend is a good softball manager or maybe a good dog trainer.

**He mows lawns for everyone in the summer and makes a lot of money. I guess that takes organization.**

Sure it does.

**He told me he's tried to do better about cleaning his room, but he just can't seem to do it.**

Organizing the Super Slob side of yourself is sort of like rubbing your stomach and patting your head at the same time. It can be done, but it isn't easy and it takes practice. Years of throwing your jacket on the floor and kicking pizza boxes under the bed can't be changed overnight. A person has to really work at changing.

When we slide into *our* Super Slobsville selves, we find that we need quick help. We need a quick trick that will give us the kick we need to get started on the three secrets! So we've scattered through this book some of our quick tricks, which we call Super Slob Tips. They don't get you organized, but they get you over the idea that you're hopeless and helpless! Here's the first one.

---

**SUPER SLOB TIP:** Throw out the old banana peels in your room and put your dirty clothes in the laundry. Set a timer for 15 minutes and work as hard as you can until you hear the buzzer. Even if you're not done, your room will look better than it did. You'll feel better than you did. Enough better to work 15 minutes more, maybe?

---

**I'm a Super Slob when it comes to school! Have you got some Super Slob Tips for me?**

Sure, but let's start with how the three secrets can get you organized to make school go easier.

# MAKING SCHOOL WORK

Getting organized can help you take charge of things at school as well as at home. Can't you just see your gym teacher's face when you start showing up on time in clean gym clothes? Or your science teacher's face when you pull out your homework—in one piece? In fact, the teachers who aren't super-organized themselves will wish they knew your secrets!

**Wow! I've got one teacher who's a real slob. She's always telling me to get organized—but you should see her desk! Wait till I tell her what her problem is.**

For goodness' sake, don't do that! You've got troubles enough already. She may be more organized than you think she is. Some people who are keepers like to work with lots of stuff on their desk, but they know where every piece of paper is and what it's for. That's why Secret #3 is so important. Everyone has to find a way that works for them—even if it looks like a mess to someone else. Your teacher has her ways. You have yours. Don't try to tell her how to get organized, or you may find yourself organizing about fifty extra math problems in her room after school!

**Just kidding. What I really need is a way to keep track of stuff. Yesterday I lost the permission slip I was supposed to take home. Today I couldn't find my math book in my locker. Some days I think I'm hopeless.**

Remember Secret #2—Take charge of your problem. Begin with your locker. Think of it as more than just a place to throw your jacket. Your locker is your home away from home. It's the place you keep everything you need to make your school day go smoothly. Stick a couple of quarters, a spare pen, and a pencil to the wall with duct tape or adhesive tape. Keep a big plastic trash bag folded flat on the shelf so that you have an extra raincoat or book cover. Add a couple of Band-Aids and some tissues, and you'll be ready for anything.

**My locker's not big enough for extra stuff. Besides, I share a locker.**

Tell your locker mate what you're doing. Divide the space so that each of you knows where your stuff goes. You can draw a chalk line down the middle, or one of you can use the top shelf and the other the floor of the locker.

Get a small basket or box that fits on the shelf of the locker and another for the floor. You can pull out the baskets, get what you want, and shove them back in easier than you can scramble through loose things.

Buy magnetic hooks to put on inside walls for hanging mittens and scarves. Put magnetic plastic baskets on the inside of the door for lightweight things. Keep one basket just for special papers like permission slips that you and your locker mate need to take home. Strips of magnets also work great for putting up pictures and posters.

If you both return books you aren't using and take home extra clothes, you'll have space for everything.

---

**SUPER SLOB TIP:** When you can find your locker by following your nose or the ant trail, toss out those old lunch bags at once. Plan a major clean-out for tomorrow.

---

### What if my locker mate won't go along with that?

If your locker mate won't go along with organizing, ask someone who will to swap locker mates. Be sure you let the school person in charge of lockers know you made the swap.

When you swap lockers (for any reason), get a new lock. You're responsible for what's in the locker. You don't want *anyone* but you and your locker mate to know your locker combination. Not even your best friend should know. Blaming someone else when things are lost or stolen is easy to do, and you could lose your friend. Even worse, if someone uses your locker, even as a joke, to store drugs or firecrackers or anything else that isn't supposed to be in school, you could get in trouble.

**I don't know about a new lock. I have trouble opening the one I have.**

Always take the time to practice with a new lock until you can open it quickly. If it won't work easily, get another one. Buy one if the school locks won't work. You have to be able to get in and out of your locker fast. You know better than we do how little time there is between classes.

**What if I can't remember my combination?**

Try turning the numbers into a silly verse you make up to fit the pattern. It might go something like: "**14** cows went to the *right,* **23** horses *left* that night. They ran to the *right* two times around. At **26** marks a door was found."

Or sing the numbers to "Jingle Bells": "**Fourteen** right, is doing fine, **twenty-three** *left* around. Two times *right* makes it mine—to **twenty-six** marks I'm bound."

**I hope nobody hears me singing that stupid song! They laugh at me enough as it is, because I'm always dropping stuff on my way to class.**

Be organized going to class, too. You don't have to walk along the halls shedding pencils and papers and books like an overloaded dump truck. Use pens and pencils with clips on them. Clip the pens and pencils to your pocket or your shirt or your notebook pages. Don't take anything around with you that you can leave in your locker. If your special project won't fit, ask a favorite teacher if you can leave it in the classroom just for the day.

**But I have to carry a bunch of books around all morning because I can't go back to my locker until lunch.**

If you don't carry a backpack, use an elastic belt or a book strap. That holds everything together. If you drop books that are strapped together, you have only one thing to pick up. The books aren't so likely to get kicked in four different directions down the hall.

In class, put the books under your seat and the strap on top of your desk.

When you get ready to leave class, you'll see the strap and remember to get the books under your seat. Slip them and your notebook back in the strap again. Be sure to put all the class papers you've been working on *inside* your notebook so that they won't get lost or messed up by the strap. If the book strap gets in your way on the desk, put it around your shoe. You'll remember it when you walk on it!

**That's another problem. I've got papers hanging out of my notebook every which way. My English teacher is on my back to get my notebook better organized. I've tried her way. But it didn't seem to help.**

Don't even try to organize your notebook just because your teacher tells you to do it.

**You mean you're telling me I don't have to do what the teacher tells me?**

Not quite! We're saying that organizing doesn't work if you do it only because someone else wants you to do it. To make organizing work, you have to figure what's in it for *you.*

**I'm not sure I understand.**

You have to see exactly how organizing makes your life easier or helps you in some way. Otherwise, getting organized and staying organized will seem like too much trouble.

For example: Did you ever lose a handout you needed? Have you ever finished homework but not been able to find it when you got to class, even though you knew you had it? Did you ever have to borrow paper from somebody else because you couldn't find a clean sheet?

**For sure!**

Then you already know that just carrying a notebook isn't enough. You know you have to have some kind of organized plan for taking care of the papers in the notebook.

Each year from now through high school, you'll find that you have more and more class notes, homework, and handouts from teachers to carry with you. You'll need a way to take care of all those papers. If your teacher's plan doesn't make sense to you, make up your own. The teacher's way is probably a good one—for her and for some students. But remember Secret #3. For you, another way may be best.

**How do I figure out my best way?**

You need to ask yourself questions like these:

- Do I want one notebook for everything, or do I want a separate notebook for each subject?
- Would spiral notebooks work better than three-ring ones for me?
- Would I be more comfortable with a clipboard and some plastic folders with pockets?
- How would I carry loose papers?
- Where would I keep homework papers—by subject, or all in one place?
- Would it help to glue a big envelope in the back of my notebook for homework papers, or would clipping a colored plastic folder into my notebook work better?
- Am I careful about putting papers back in a notebook, or do I need a place I can just stash them until I get home and sort them?

**Gee, I never thought of using anything but what I have.**
Don't think you have to settle for the first thing you find in the drugstore either. If it's okay with your folks (and the school doesn't tell you what to buy), check out department stores, catalogs, gift shops, printing places, and office supply stores. You'll find dozens of different kinds of notebooks, organizers, pads, and folders. They come in every color and shape.

If you feel better carrying something that other students at your school use, check out how friends who make good grades carry papers to school. Work out a system that is sort of like theirs, but make it right for you.

**But what will my English teacher say?**
Talk with her. She may have a special reason for wanting the papers for her class organized a certain way. Or she may

just be trying to get her students to organize, and she's showing them the way she finds easiest.

If you show her a neat notebook and explain why you organized it as you did, she may go along with you. At least she'll be impressed that you're thinking!

**But what if she won't go along with my way?**

If she doesn't go along with you, do it her way. When you need to follow someone else's system, ask them to break down their system into small steps, just like in Secret #1. Then follow it one step at a time. Their system may be harder to follow at first, but you might find you like it after you try it.

Using another person's system may be more work for you, but you can do it if passing a course is important to you. And remember, you won't be in that class forever.

---

**SUPER SLOB TIP:** To put your notebook in order, make a deal with a friend who finds organizing easy.

---

**Papers aren't the only thing I have trouble keeping track of. Some days when we have a late start or an assembly, some classes are dropped. Then I forget which class I'm supposed to go to.**

Why not tape a copy of your schedule inside your notebook cover? Include room numbers and a list of how times change on special days. You could even make a map of the school showing your classrooms. (When you see that other kids are lost, you can be the cool one and show them where to go.) Decorate the schedule and map with drawings or stickers.

Make your notebook work for you. Don't let it be something you drag to class because you have to. Make it funny or clever or pretty. Use colored markers or stickers or photographs under clear Contact paper. Make it *you.* Then you'll *want* to remember to take it around with you.

**This kid that sits next to me drew a marijuana picture on the back of his notebook and put the names of all the drugs we learned about in drug ed in funny printing.**

Doesn't that make you think he uses drugs? He may or may not, but that's what people are going to think. So be careful what you put on your folder. People will look at your decorations and make judgments about you. If you put four-letter words or booze bottles or sexy pictures on your notebook, most kids will think, "What a show-off," even if they laugh. And teachers may think you've got a problem.

Also, think twice before you put a special friend's name or initials on your notebook. If you change your mind, you're stuck with what you wrote for the life of the notebook. If you want to put names on your notebook, put them on tape or labels that peel off!

And while we're talking about names, be *sure* to put your

name, address, and phone number on the inside cover of *every* notebook you use. Add the words "Please Return!" You spend a lot of time taking notes. If you lose a notebook, the papers you lose could make the difference in whether you pass or fail a course.

**Okay. I can see how having an organized notebook will keep me from losing papers, but it won't help me remember when I'm supposed to turn stuff in to the teacher. I forgot a book report last week.**

Having a way to keep track of what you are supposed to do is every bit as important as your notebook. You need some way to remember your homework assignments, when projects are due, what tests are coming up, and when you need to return library books. We don't know of anything more important, but many students tell us they have a hard time doing it.

**My mom gave me a weekly calendar book from her office, but I don't want to carry it around. I'd feel stupid taking it out and writing in it.**

You keep forgetting Secret #3! You have to find a way to keep track of what you need to do in a way that works for you. That means you find a way that doesn't make you feel dopey doing it. Let's look at the problem. How do you try to remember what homework to do?

**I just try to remember. Sometimes I write it down on a piece of paper.**

Does that work?

**Sometimes.**

Sometimes isn't good enough. Suppose the head of the cafeteria remembers to buy milk "sometimes". If you eat in the cafeteria every day and like milk, you wouldn't think "sometimes" is okay. You need a simple system to keep track of everything every day.

You can easily keep track of your assignments if you make up a RAP (Reports, Assignments, and Projects) sheet. A RAP sheet is a kind of school calendar for reminding you what you have to do. You may want one sheet for each day or one for the week to keep in your notebook. Do whichever works best for you. Put it where you can find it easily. When the teacher gives an assignment, flip right to it.

We've given you a couple of sample RAP sheets in the Appendix, but use your imagination. Put drawings on yours, or decorate it with stickers. Maybe you can make yours on a computer and store it on a disk so that you can print one out whenever you need it. You might want to put it on colored paper so that you can find it easily.

If you like one of our designs, copy it on a copying machine. Punch holes in each sheet, or staple them to your folder. Keep plenty of extra sheets on hand. The RAP sheets will tell you what to do and when to do it.

**So how is that better than writing it on a piece of paper?**

You won't have to turn all your pockets inside out to look for the paper with the assignment on it. Also, you won't waste time reading the wrong chapter if you can't find that piece of paper.

---

**SUPER SLOB TIP:** As soon as you get schoolbooks, put a couple of pull-off sticky labels on the inside back cover of each one. Write the assignments on the labels. Be sure to remove the labels from those books at the end of the year.

---

**I guess I see how getting organized can help me keep track of my stuff and what homework I'm supposed to do. But can it help me *do* my homework?**

It can help you not only with your homework, but also in your class work and tests. The next chapter tells you how.

# PLANNING TO STUDY

The three secrets still apply when you're organizing school-work. You need to break big jobs down into small ones, remind yourself that you can do the jobs, and then find your own special way of doing them.

**How can I use them when I study?**
How do you study now?

**I just read the chapter and try to remember what it says.**
**Reading is reading. I don't see how you can organize it.**
You can read better and faster and remember more of what

you read if you use Secret #1. Break your reading down into small steps. The first step is to ask yourself these questions:

- How much do I already know about this? Have I visited this place, read a story by this same author, seen a TV show or movie about the same subject, studied it before (and so on)?
- What do I want to get out of my reading? Am I looking for certain facts or why something happened or the theme of a story or something else?

**Then what?**

Skim through the chapter (or the book) before you start to read. Check out the pictures. Do key words or names or dates jump out at you in headings or in pictures? Make a mental map of the chapter. Where does it start? Where does it seem to go? Where does it end?

Skim the first and last paragraphs of each chapter. They often sum up the chapter.

Now concentrate on the reading. Don't reread lines over and over because you aren't concentrating. Go slowly enough to understand what you read. But don't go so slowly that you let your mind drift away.

Finally, ask yourself as you go along if you understand what you are reading. If you don't, then go back and reread. To help make sense of it, try to tie in the new information with information you already know. Some people find it helps to jot down new words or a few notes as they read.

**That sounds like a lot of work.**

You'll find that reading this way organizes your thoughts as you go along. You'll remember much more of what you read.

Soon you'll do it out of habit and you won't think of it as work.

---

**SUPER SLOB TIP:** If time is short, here's how to get the most from the time you have. Read all headings in dark type. Read captions under graphs, maps, and pictures. Then be sure you understand the first and last paragraphs of the chapter and the summary, if there is one. You'll at least know what the chapter is about.

---

**My teacher says I need to organize my thoughts when I write reports, too, but that doesn't make sense to me. I have a report that's due in two weeks and I've thought and thought, but I haven't come up with anything.**

Organizing your thoughts for a report is more than just thinking about something. Before you can organize your thoughts for a paper, you need the right thoughts to think about! Let's look at how you can go about getting some thoughts to organize for your paper.

### What do I do first?

You need to start with a topic.

**My teacher gave us a list of topics we can use if we want to, but I didn't like any of them.**

You'll do better on your report if you pick a topic that interests you.

**I'm trying to talk my folks into getting another dog.**

Good. Why don't you write something about dogs? *Dogs* is

a big subject, though. Lots of books have been written about dogs. Can you cut the topic down (English teachers call it "limiting the topic") to just one small thing about dogs?

**What about how to take care of a puppy?**

That's good for now. Once you get farther along on the paper, you may want to limit it even more—perhaps how to train a puppy, or when to see a vet for shots. But to start, ask yourself, "What would I like to know about taking care of a puppy?"

**I guess I'd like to know how old a puppy has to be before you can take it home, and what to feed it. Oh, and how to teach it not to mess on the floor. And how to get it to come when I call it, and how to teach it tricks.**

Turn each of those statements into a question, and write them down.

1. How old must a puppy be to leave its mother?
2. What does a puppy eat?
3. How is a puppy housebroken?
4. How is a puppy trained to follow commands?
5. How is a puppy trained to do tricks?

As you read books or talk to people, you will be looking for answers to these questions. You also may find some good information about a question you didn't think to ask. You can add to your list of questions. By making this list of questions and taking notes, you are collecting (or organizing) your thoughts about puppies. You've used Secret #1 to break down the large topic into small ones.

Now you need to start finding out all you can about taking care of a puppy.

**My friend has a couple of books on pets. I can borrow them.**

That's a good place to start. You could also visit your local library and your school library. Librarians may be able to find other books that you don't see on the shelves. They also have videos, movies, and film strips. And they can show you where to find articles in newspapers and magazines.

Next, think about all the other places you can get information.

**What kinds of places?**

Write to companies that make pet food to get free booklets. Call a veterinarian's office to find the names and addresses of other companies you can write to for free information. Getting information by mail takes time, so you have to get started on mail orders as soon as you decide on your topic. If your paper is due in two weeks, you won't have time to write for information this time. What else can you do?

**How about talking to a vet?**

Now you're getting the idea. Call to make an appointment. Tell why you want to talk to him or her.

**I guess I should write down what the vet says. I'll never remember it all.**

Begin taking notes just as soon as you get any information, whether it's from a book or from talking to an expert. You can use a notebook or index cards. Most people find that index cards are better because they're easy to shuffle and move around when you're ready to write the paper. Put a rubber band around the cards to keep them together. If you decide to use a notebook, think "sheets of paper" from now on when we say "cards."

---

**SUPER SLOB TIP:** If you're likely to drop or lose the cards, buy the cards in a spiral binding or use a spiral-bound notebook. Put your name and address and "Please Return!" on the outside card or cover.

---

At the top of each card, jot down which question the card is about. Since you numbered your questions when you listed them, just put the number of the question at the top. Then write where (newspaper, interview, book) you found the information. Under that heading, write *in your own words* ONE piece of information. Whether you're interviewing someone or using books or other sources, take notes the same way.

On your note card, sum up what is said in only a few words. That means write down the main idea. If you copy exactly what a person or book says, put it in quote marks to show that someone else said it. Save exact quotes for one or two things that add special interest to your report.

Use abbreviations or short ways of writing a word. For instance, "&" is a short way to write the word "and"; use "vet" instead of writing out "veterinarian." Leave out words like "the" and "a" that don't add to the meaning.

Here's a sample note card:

---

#4          *Dog News Digest*, pp. 22–23          April, 1989

To control dog, talk with firm voice & spank gently on rump.

"Never hit him hard enough to really hurt him." (quote from Dr. Alan Smart, Northeast Dog Training School)

---

**Why put only one thing on a card? I can get a lot more on it.**

Because after you write all your cards, you will sort them into piles by question. See how many cards of information you have on each question. If you have more than one idea on a card, you'll get confused about which part of a card goes with which question. If you don't have many cards for a question, you will know that you don't have much information on that question. Then you can go back and look in some other places until you have all you want.

---

**SUPER SLOB TIP:** If you have enough information on all but one or two questions, and your report-writing time runs out, toss out those questions.

---

**When I think I have enough cards, what do I do then?**

Decide in what order you want to answer the questions. Put the cards in that order.

**That seems like a lot of work, and I still have to write the paper.**

The paper will practically write itself, because all your information and thoughts are organized!

First, you'll need an introduction. That's a paragraph that tells what you're going to write about in the report. It will use the questions you've asked. Your paragraph might say something like this:

*This report will talk about raising a puppy. It will tell you when a puppy can leave its mother, what a puppy eats, how to housebreak a puppy, and how to train it to follow commands and do tricks.*

Now go from one card to the next. Turn what you have on each one into a full sentence. Don't forget to change the abbreviations back into words.

At the end of your paper, write a paragraph that is much the same as the introduction. Use slightly different words to sum up what you talked about in your report. In this case, your last paragraph would be what you decided was important about the care and training of puppies based on what you learned.

**I wish I didn't have to write my report. I find talking easier than writing.**

Then try this: Organize the cards in the order you want. Using the cards, talk your report into a tape recorder. Then write the report by copying down your words from the tape.

Read through and make any changes you need to make.

**I don't have very good handwriting and I'm a bad speller.**

Ask your teacher if you can have someone type your paper and take care of spelling errors.

If the teacher says you have to do the work yourself, write slowly and as carefully as you can. Take your time.

There are special dictionaries that can help you, too. They don't give the meanings of words. They list the correct spelling of a word in one color ink and wrong ways people might spell the word in another color ink. That's a big help when you don't know how to find a word in a regular dictionary. Check at your library or local bookstore.

You can solve both your spelling and handwriting problems if you learn to type your paper on a computer that has a spelling checker. That's easiest of all. Lots of schools and libraries have computers that you can use.

**And then use a beeper to remember to turn my paper in when it's due, right?**

Yes, but don't forget to check your paper before you turn

it in even if someone else typed it. You are responsible for your report, and the typist could have made some mistakes.

Be sure that the punctuation and grammar are correct. They are important to the organization of your paper, too. They help make clear to the reader what you're trying to say.

### Should I take notes in class on cards, too?

A better way to take class notes is to organize your notes on a sheet of paper. Here's one way:

1. Draw a vertical line about two inches from the left edge of your paper from top to bottom.
2. Put the topic your teacher is talking about and the date in the upper right corner of the paper.
3. When you take notes, write them in the large space to the right of the line you drew. Use few words. Use "&" instead of "and." Use capital letters to stand for words used over and over. For example, use "RE" to stand for "Roman Empire." Use symbols like "$" for "money" or "yrs" for "years." Underline or star (∗) points your teacher says are very important.
4. To further organize your notes, look them over when you do your homework. Then write a word or phrase in the space on the left that tells or sums up what the notes on the right are about.
5. When you study, you can quickly find the notes you want by glancing through the words on the left. To study for a test, cover up the section on the right. Then ask yourself what you remember about the words or phrases on the left. If the test is only on vocabulary, cover the left

side of the page and try to recall those words by reading their definitions.

Remember, don't try to write down everything—just the important points. You can look up details in your book.

**I still have trouble knowing what the teacher thinks is important. It all sounds alike to me. So I copy down as much as I can. Sometimes I'm so busy writing, that I don't hear the next thing the teacher says, and it turns out to be the most important part. Then when it's time for a test, I ask my friends what they're going to study.**

Most teachers try to help you know what's important, but you have to know what to look and listen for. Some teachers write objectives on the board. The objectives tell you the main ideas the teacher wants you to think about that day. Other teachers start the class period by telling you in a few words what is important. Some will end the class by telling you what *was* important in the lesson. So listen very carefully at those times. Learn each teacher's style.

**What do you mean by style?**

For example, with teachers who rarely write anything on the blackboard, pay very close attention to anything they do write on the board. It's likely to be important. On the other hand, if the teacher is always writing on the blackboard, copy down anything that is underlined or starred.

You also need to learn teachers' "pointer" words and phrases that they use when something is important. They will use words like "notice," "remember," "important," "don't forget," and especially, "This will be on the test." Those words and phrases point to the things you need to take notes on and remember.

Teachers also show you by their actions. Maybe they get closer to you and their voice gets higher. Or they wave their hands. Or maybe they drop their voice and pound on the table. Study each of your teachers to learn how their behavior patterns tell you what's important to them. You will also find that their tests are usually made up of the points that they think are most important.

**You haven't said anything about how to get organized for math class.**

We haven't said anything about math because we are sure your math teachers have already had a lot to say about it! Math *is* the organizing of number facts. To do well in math you *must* be neat and careful.

If you have a hard time keeping numbers in the proper columns, buy some graph paper with big squares. Write one number in each square and use the lines to help you keep the numbers straight.

Because each step in math depends on your knowing the steps that came before, you mustn't skip any steps. For example, you don't learn dividing fractions until you learn to add them. So if you have to miss math class for more than a couple of days, *always* ask for some catch-up help from your teacher or another student who is good at math. Otherwise you'll have a hard time with the next test.

**I could sure use some help on taking tests. I get nervous**

**and mess up on tests, even when I study.**

Maybe you need to organize your test taking, too. Here's how.

First read all the directions. Be sure you know what you are supposed to do. Remind yourself that you've been in school for a lot of years now and that you've passed a lot of tests.

Next, look at the questions one at a time. Answer the easiest ones first, if you like. (Remember? Do it your way.) Then go back and look at the others one at a time. If it's a math test, break each problem down into the steps you need to do to find the answer. Solve it one step at a time.

If you can't answer a question—go on to the next one. Think about the ones you've already answered. Do they give you any clues about some of the harder ones?

**Sometimes I make a lot of dumb mistakes on a test. What can I do about that?**

When you finish any test, if you have time, go back and be sure that your answers make sense. On a math test, check your computations to be sure that you didn't add 2 and 3 and get 6, or subtract when you should have added.

On word problems or essay questions, be sure you answered the questions that were asked. For example, if the English teacher asked you to describe your favorite character in a book, did you instead tell why the book was your favorite? If you did, just draw a slanting line through your whole answer. Don't scratch the answer out or try to erase it. That wastes your time. Put a note at the top of your answer saying, "See the end of the test." At the end of the test, write the answer you were supposed to write the first time.

The key to good test taking is organized studying, reading the test directions carefully, thinking about the questions, thinking about your answers, and keeping track of your time if it's a timed test. Most important of all is staying cool and not panicking! Remember Secret #2. You *can* take control and be in charge!

### Keeping track of time is hard for me.

If you're talking about test taking, take a look before you start at how many questions you need to answer in the time you have. When you've done half that number, look at the clock to see if you must speed up.

If you're talking about how you use the hours you have every day, use the three secrets to help you keep track of your time. Knowing where your time goes can make life much easier for you. Let's talk about it.

# TAKING YOUR TIME

Even though school may seem to go on forever, you have many hours in your day when you aren't in school. How do you organize your after-school time?

**I don't even want to think about getting organized after school. I just want to have fun. But I do have a few things I have to do.**

Some organization might help you have more time for fun. Just what do you do after school?

Sometimes I stay at school for a club meeting. And once in a while I go to the store with a friend to buy shampoo and stuff. Mostly my friends and I watch TV and listen to music or talk. Then there's music lessons and practice. In the spring I play softball. I also have things Mom wants me to do, like carrying out the trash, setting the table for dinner, and stacking the dishwasher afterward. Sometimes I have to cook dinner, too.

Whew! We're tired just hearing what you do. By the way, you forgot to mention homework.

**Oh, yeah. I guess I do have that, too. Maybe a little organizing wouldn't hurt. How do I start?**

It sounds like you need to fit a lot of things into a busy day. To organize time, you need to know about *priorities.* Priorities are the things you absolutely *have* to do. You have to make sure you find time to do them. Then you do other things in the time left over. What's the most important thing you have to do every day when you get home from school?

**I suppose my homework is number one—even if I forgot to say it.**

That sounds right.

**My mom counts on me helping around the house, too.**

Then that is a top priority, too. Why don't you make a list to see what your priorities look like. Put "homework" as number one and "helping Mom" as number two. Then put down all the other things you have to do and want to do in the order of their importance.

### Once I have my list, then what?

You will decide how much time you need for the things you absolutely *have* to do, like homework and helping your mom. Then you decide on the time of day when you'll do them.

### When do I fit in what *I* want to do? And how about music and softball and all the other things?

Decide that with the help of your family. When you were very little, your parents decided on your priorities. For the most part, they still do. But each year that you get older, you will have to make more and more decisions about what's important to you. Therefore, you'll make better decisions if you begin to understand and help select the priorities in your life now.

### Mom wants me to do my homework as soon as I get home from school, but I just waste my time. I can't concentrate until later in the evening.

People are very different when it comes to work time. Some people are at their best and ready to go in midafternoon. They do their studies and have the rest of the day with no worries. Other people work better after eating dinner or even later. A few people are early-morning people. They go to bed early and get up in the morning and do their homework an hour or two before school.

Talk to your mom and ask her to let you try it your way for two weeks. Set a time to do homework, and do it every day at that time for two weeks.

### If I set an exact time, I'd never remember it.

If you had an uncle coming over at five o'clock to give you a hundred dollars, would you remember the time?

**You bet!**

You remember what you *want* to remember. We all do. If we want to get out of doing something, we "forget" it.

To keep track of time, buy a watch that has an alarm on it. Set the alarm to go off at homework time every day. After a week or two of this, you'll be in the habit.

**But suppose a friend calls during that time?**

Tell your friend you can't talk now. You don't have to give a reason if you don't want to. If your friend asks why, simply say, "I've got some things I have to do before dinner (or bed, or going skating, etc.)."

**Some nights I don't have any homework, so I can goof off then, right?**

What about that book you need to read for a book report? And have you finished your science project? Those are homework, too, even if the teacher didn't mention them in school today. But if you truly don't have any homework, then enjoy!

**Besides, I don't know anybody who does homework *every* night.**

Not *anybody*?

**Maybe some of the older kids.**

Why do you suppose they do it?

**Maybe doing homework and being organized gets easier to do when you're older?**

Not really. Older kids are just more likely to have learned the hard way that they need to plan and organize and do what they need to do.

Growing up doesn't happen all at once. You grow up a step or two at a time. When you were little, grown-ups did all your planning and organizing for you. They told you when you could eat, when you could sleep, where to store your toys, and when you would go to school. You didn't have to be organized. But think how much stuff you have and how many things you do now that you didn't when you were five.

By the time you graduate from high school, you will have many more things to plan and organize. That's why it's important to learn organizing now. Lots of grown-ups have never learned what you know, just from reading this book, about *how* and *why* they should organize.

**I never thought of that before. But sometimes, even though I know I should, I just don't *feel* like doing my homework.**

Remember Secret #2. When it is time to do your homework (or anything else you need to do), count to ten to remind yourself that you can do it.

Next, sit down at your desk. Say to yourself, "If I were going to do my homework, what would I do first?" Then start that first thing. By the time you do that one, you'll be well on your way. You can't wait until you "feel like" doing it, because you may never "feel like it"!

**But what should I do *first*?**

That's where your homework sheet that you filled out during school helps. Look at your sheet(s) and see what you have to do. Most people start with the hardest job before they get too tired. Other people like to start with an easy job to get them started. Try and see which way works best for you.

If you have an extra lot of homework and you have a study period the next day, do the homework first for the classes that come before the study period. Then you can finish work for the later classes in study period.

When you study for tests, study a little, then do some other homework, and then go back to studying. You will learn more by spacing out your learning. Spaced learning also works better if you have to memorize something.

When you finish an assignment, draw a line through it on your homework sheet. Crossing out an item makes you feel good!

**Everyday things aren't the only things I have to do. How can I remember to do things like going to the dentist?**

There's still nothing better than a large calendar—one with lots of space to write in. Write on it all the special things you have to do. First, mark the days that you regularly have to be somewhere. If you get your braces fixed every other Wednesday, go through the calendar and mark every other Wednesday with a big B (for Braces). Look at your RAP sheets and write down the due dates of any big projects. Write down when exams come. List school holidays, sports, special days. Put a big circle around your birthday! Use stickers, if you like.

Be sure to keep a record on your calendar of the days you

were absent from school or late and you had an excuse. Put A for absent and L for late. Sometimes school records get messed up and you need your own records to show what days you were excused.

Let the calendar keep track for you. Then you don't have to remember lots of little things. You just have to remember one thing—to look at the calendar.

**I forget to look at a calendar.**

Get in the habit of checking what's on for the next day as soon as you get up from dinner at night. That way you still have time to do some special project you might have forgotten.

Sunday night is a good time to check what you need to do in the upcoming week. That helps you organize your time priorities for the week. For example, if you have a hard test scheduled for Wednesday, don't plan to spend Tuesday afternoon shopping at the mall.

Be sure to put new things on the calendar when you learn about them at school or at home. Do that when you check the calendar for the next day or week.

**Even if I put the due date for a report on the calendar, it won't help me much. I'm sort of a "last-minute" person. I find it hard to do a project until the day before it's due. Then I work late that night. I know that's not right, but that's the way I work best.**

Are you really a "last-minute" person? Most true "last-minute" people have actually been thinking about the project for days. When the time comes to do it, they do a pretty good job.

Or do you just put off work until the last day because you don't want to do it, and end up doing a poor job? Be honest with yourself.

If you really are a "last-minute" person, here are some tips that will help you. A few days before the project is due, at least get together everything you're going to need: books, cardboard, paint, staples, paper, etc. Start thinking about the project. Take notes on what you want to do. When an idea pops in your mind, jot it down. Then when report-day-minus-one comes, you will probably be able to finish on time.

Try to learn to do some of your work earlier. One day you will simply have too many things to do, and you won't have enough hours to finish on time.

**How do I get myself to do things earlier?**

Putting "Warning—Report Due" markers on your calendar a couple of days ahead helps.

Some people find that "self-talking" also helps you get started. When you are taking your shower in the morning or getting dressed, talk to yourself about your day. Think about what you would like to get done that day, and then picture yourself doing it. For example, suppose you need to start that project. Picture yourself getting up from lunch at school and saying to your friends, "I gotta go. See you later." Then imagine yourself going straight to the media center and starting your project. Picture that great librarian helping you get off to a super start.

When you actually finish lunch at school that day, open your mouth and say, "I gotta go. See you later." Then head for the media center. You'll find it easier to leave your friends and get to work if you have a plan.

**I'm not only late doing things, I'm usually late getting places, too. I always think I have more time than I do.**

One way to get to a place on time is to organize backward from the time you have to be there. Say you have to be at the dentist at 5:30. Allow yourself time for a drink of water or going to the bathroom after you get there, so plan on being five minutes early (5:25). Now figure how long it takes the bus to get you there. Fifteen minutes? Don't forget having to wait for it, so you'd better allow another five minutes (5:05). What do you have to do before you leave? Walk the dog? There's another ten minutes (4:55). Don't forget to brush your teeth, comb your hair, and find your bus fare (4:45). Now plan on an extra five minutes in case the phone rings. You can be pretty sure of getting to the dentist on time if you start getting ready to go at 4:40.

**I never thought of planning backward before. That might work, but something always seems to come up that I didn't plan on.**

That happens to all of us, so most people allow even more time if they absolutely, positively *have* to be someplace on time—like catching a plane.

**What about being late to class? There isn't enough time between classes to do all I have to do.**

If you plan ahead, there's usually enough time to go to your locker and see teachers. Most people are late, though, because they're talking with friends. This is often true if you have a best friend that you meet between classes. There's *never* enough time to say all you want to say.

So take turns keeping track of the time. One week, you be the one to keep track and remind your friend it's time to go to class. The next week, your friend will remind you.

**Some of my friends seem to get a lot more done between classes and during the school day than I do. How do they do it?**

People have different energy levels. Some people are able to live at a faster pace. They are the ones who rush down the halls and do two or three things at a time. Other people need to concentrate on one thing at a time.

**I wish I had been born with a lot of energy and could do a bunch of things at one time.**

Getting good food and good exercise every day may increase your energy. Talk to your school nurse or doctor about this.

As for doing two things at once, try these tricks:

•   Do mindless things like cleaning your shoes or exercising while you watch TV.

•   Do one-handed jobs like sorting a desk drawer while you talk on the phone.
•   Swap jobs with a friend. Are you quick at raking leaves but not at washing windows, while your friend is the opposite? Ask your folks if you can rake leaves at both houses while your friend washes windows.
•   While you ride the bus or wait for others, do some of your homework. Carry a piece of paper and a pencil with you, and start a book report or outline a science project. Carry a paperback so that you can read that novel for English, or listen to a taped book on a small recorder.
•   When you know you may be waiting a long time (like in a doctor's office) take along some paper and a pen, and write your aunt and thank her for her present. Never mind that it was weeks or months ago. While you are at it, write to your old friend who moved away.
•   Time yourself on jobs like emptying the dishwasher or starting a load of laundry. Often these jobs take a much

shorter time than you think. You can do them while you are waiting for your bread to toast or for your sister to get her coat and start the car.

**I'm going to try some of those ideas. But I've already learned that no matter how hard I try, I can't be organized all the time. Do some people find it easier to get organized than others?**

That seems to be true. A few people seem to be organized from the time they are little kids. Most people have to work a little at getting organized. A few people—perhaps some with a serious learning disability or other special problem—have a very hard time. But everyone can do better if they try.

**Sometimes I just don't feel like trying.**

There are lots of good reasons why you might feel that way. Let's look at some of them.

# TROUBLESHOOTING

How come I'm broke already?

Sometimes knowing the secrets of getting organized isn't enough. Getting organized is hard when other problems get in your way. Then organizing seems like "too much trouble."

**I know what you mean. Sometimes I get busy with a lot of things and leave my room in a mess for days. If I leave it long enough, my mom cleans it for me. She fusses and I feel guilty, but I like having her do it.**

That means she's still treating you like a little kid. Every time you get someone to clean up your mess for you, you're saying, "I'm still a baby." Is that how you think about your-self?


**No way! I'm no baby. But my mom does treat me like one sometimes. Every night Mom says, "Do your homework before you watch TV"—even when I've already done my homework. Or she comes in my room and moves my stuff around without asking me.**

Being in charge of what you do (Secret #2) isn't easy to carry out when your folks still think of you as a little kid. If you're serious about taking charge of your life, talk with your folks. Tell them why you want to be trusted to do your jobs without their nagging you. Point out how much better you are doing and how much you want to be in charge of your room and your schoolwork. Tell them you know you won't be perfect, but you will try to keep things better than you have before.

They'll be surprised and pleased. They may not believe you if you've made promises in the past and not lived up to them. You'll just have to prove to them that you've grown up enough to do it right this time.


**I just wish my folks wouldn't nag me about my room. It's my room and I should be able to keep it the way I want.**

Everyone wants control of their own space. This makes for a problem sometimes when kids begin to grow up and want more control.

It is natural for you to want a place where you can keep your personal things.

**Then what can I do?**

Start by offering a deal to your folks. Tell them that you'll work hard to keep your room neater (not perfect, mind you—just better) if they won't fuss at you about your room for two weeks. Ask them what three things bother them the most, and agree to work on those things. Maybe it's that you and your friend eat cookies in your room and leave crumbs everywhere. Or you toss your dirty clothes on the floor, or play music too loud at night.

Whatever the three things are, do your best to keep your end of the deal. Keep remembering how much you want to be left alone.

**Sometimes I get so mad at my folks when they do something like keeping me from going to a game that I don't want to get organized or do good in school or anything.**

Keeping a messy room or failing in math is one way of dealing with angry feelings. And may hurt your folks. But it hurts you even more than it hurts them. You're the one who has to live in the pigpen or go to summer school if you fail a class.

**What can I do, then?**

Talk to your folks and tell them what you're upset about—whether it's a little thing or a big thing. Ask them to help you find a way to deal with your problem.

**I don't want to just deal with my problems. I want to solve them.**

You can't solve all problems. Sometimes you simply have to learn to live with them.

Don't forget, you can use the three secrets of organization to help you decide how to deal with situations or problems that arise. If you are wondering whether to baby-sit for a neighbor, you need to know how late you'd stay, what you'd be doing, when you'd do your homework, how much money you'd get, and so on.

If you're considering skipping school, you have to think about what the teacher will do, how you can make up the class, what your parents would say if they caught you, and so on.

**Then what?**

Based on your answers to those questions, you take charge of what you want to do (Secret #2) and do what's right for *you* (Secret #3), even if it doesn't make your neighbor or friends happy.

If you don't know what to do about a problem, talk to a school counselor or a minister or rabbi.

Also ask your librarian to help you find some books on your problem. There are excellent books that can help you understand almost anything—from death and divorce to buying clothes and baking bread.

**What about books on how to save money? I never have enough. Don't tell me organization will help me there, too?**

Yes, there are books on how to save money. But here is an extra secret just for money organization.

SECRET #4 (the last one we have to tell you) is: *Save some money every time you get any.*

**No way can I save money. I never have enough as it is!**

We've said the same thing. But the truth is, if we save even a little money *just as soon as we get it*, we never miss it. The little bit saved each time adds up, and when we need to buy something big or treat ourselves to something special, the money is there.

**I'd be tempted to spend it if I did save it.**

Put it in a bank—a piggy bank that's hard to open or, better yet, a real bank.

A real bank is better because getting money out is more difficult. Also, if you put your money in a savings account, no matter how little you have, you get interest. Interest is money banks give you for using your money while you leave it with them.

**I don't know—my folks usually give me more money if I want something real bad and beg a lot!**

Think about Secret #2—take charge of your own life. That includes money. If you take charge of your money, you'll always have some to spend without having to beg. Knowing you have your own savings account gives you a really special feeling.

**How can I keep track of the rest of my money? I spend it as fast as I get it.**

We like to use envelopes to control how to use the rest of our money that we don't put in savings.

**How does that work?**

If you get money once a week, you have to plan how to make your money last all week. If you don't plan, you'll spend it in a day or two if you are like us. So here's a way to manage your money.

As soon as you get your money, set aside the amount for savings. Then put the rest of your money in envelopes. For example, if you have to have money for lunch every day, mark one envelope "Lunch." Put the exact amount of lunch money you'll need until you get paid again in that envelope. If you have to have bus money, mark another envelope "Bus," and put in all the bus money you'll need. The ones marked "Clothes" and "Gifts" can be added to each time until you need

to buy new jeans or a birthday gift. But put something in each envelope because that time *will* come. The money that's left over can be spent or saved for whatever you want.

Keep the envelopes in a safe place, and take money out only as you need it. Don't carry the envelopes around with you. You might lose them or be tempted to "borrow" from them. Don't *ever* take them to school or show them to your friends. Your money is your private business. Keep it that way.

**I'll try the envelopes, but I don't think they'll work magic. Something usually comes along that I didn't expect and I'll need more money.**

The envelopes really will help, but you're right. They aren't magic. No matter how well organized you are, things can happen that mess you up. You can try to save money, but your bicycle gets a flat tire and you have to buy a new one so that you can do your paper route.

Being organized doesn't mean living in perfect order with nothing going wrong. In fact, you have to be prepared for things to go wrong, and you can't go to pieces when that happens.

**It really makes me mad when I've worked hard to get organized and things go wrong. If I do something like spill juice on my homework, I just want to tear up my homework and forget it.**

When your organization system breaks down, try to rescue it. There are often many ways to handle a bad situation. For example, suppose you spilled grape juice on your homework. You grab a paper towel and try to clean the homework:

If you can save all but one or two pages, copy the messy ones over.

If they're a total mess but you can read through the juice, let them dry. Then iron each page between two sheets of paper towels. (Don't let the iron get too hot.) Turn the purple pages in and hope for the best!

If you can't read them at all, relax, put it out of your mind, and do the paper over tomorrow.

**Suppose it's a big report for English that has to be neat and is due the next day?**

You could take the messy papers to your teacher and show that you had finished the work and ask for more time to copy it. Most teachers will give you the extra time.

**But suppose the teacher won't?**

That could happen. Life isn't always fair. When bad things happen, do the best you can. Then play some music, ride your bike, write a poem, talk to a friend, hit some tennis balls. Work out your feelings in some safe way.

Sometimes, too, what looks like a terrible mess one moment can even turn out to be okay the next. Maybe by the end of class the teacher will have thought better of your offer to copy and will give you the extra time. But if not, get on with the rest of your life and put the bad time behind you.

**Then why bother to get organized in the first place, since so many things can happen to mess up plans?**

Sure, there are times when everything falls apart. But when you try to keep things under control, you can feel more relaxed and have more fun. You don't waste time looking for lost socks. You don't go to school with a sick feeling in your stomach because you don't have your homework. You feel good about yourself most of the time because you know what you are doing and why you are doing it.

**I like feeling that way. I keep trying to get organized and I'm making some changes, but I still have a long way to go.**
Be proud of yourself for making some changes. Don't put yourself down. Nobody's perfect—never will be. We still get in a hurry and stuff things in drawers or leave dirty dishes in the sink. Everybody does. But the important thing is that you try to live your life the best way you can. Trying to keep organized can help you do that.

Keep up the good work. You're on the right track.

# FINISHING TOUCHES

Getting organized gives you both time and money for *Finishing Touches. Finishing Touches* are all those little extras in life that make it special. They are the posters on your wall, new storage places, party plans. Use your new organization skills to carry them out.

Here are lots of *Finishing Touches.* We hope that they will help you think of some of your own.

### Your Room

*Re-arranging Your Room:*
When you want to change your room or add furniture, do

as the interior designers do. They make a drawing of a room and try out different furniture arrangements. Here's how you can do that.

On page 87 you will see a page drawn in squares. Each square stands for 1 square foot. On the page after that, you will see furniture symbols drawn to the same scale. Take both pages to a copy machine and copy them. Try to find a machine that will enlarge them.

Draw the outline of your room on the page with the squares. (If you've forgotten how to measure the square feet in your room, go back and ask your math teacher to show you.) Don't forget to note where your closet and doors and windows go. Use double lines to show where to put them.

Next, cut out the pieces of furniture that are most like the ones you have or like the ones you want. Now you can arrange them and re-arrange them until you get them just right. This will help you change your room around or save you buying furniture that won't fit.

*New Furniture:*

When you need new furniture but think you can't afford it, here are some ways to get some.

1. Ask everybody in your family to give you only one gift for your birthday (or some other special day). Ask them all to chip in and buy the piece you want. It isn't okay to ask your friends to do this.

2. Look for used furniture. Go to yard sales and second-hand furniture stores. Be sure you know how much new beds cost so that you will know if you are really getting a bargain. Check for chips and scars. Little ones

are no problem, but big ones should make you think that the furniture has been badly treated. Be sure it is still sturdy.

You can also check the "For Sale" column of a local newspaper or the community bulletin board in a grocery store. You might put an ad on the bulletin board that says you're looking for bunk beds or whatever. Ask your folks first, though, because you'll have to give your home phone number and they may not want that.

3. Ask your folks if they can meet you halfway on the cost. Then save for it.

4. Give old furniture new uses:
   a. Paint an old toy box and turn it into your "junk" box. You can throw everything in it that doesn't have a place of its own.
   b. Use a small, rickety stepladder that isn't safe to stand on anymore to hold plants or shoes.
   c. Turn a file cabinet and a small chest into a desk by placing an old door across them. To get them the same height, use bricks or pieces of wood. Cover the door and the bricks or wood with Contact paper.
   d. Use concrete blocks and planks to make more bookshelves.
   e. Cover grocery-store boxes with wallpaper remnants to use as storage boxes. Old rolls of wallpaper don't cost much in wallpaper stores.
   f. Use the good parts of worn-out sheets to make sacks to hold out-of-season clothes.
   g. Use stacks of plastic crates to make more bookshelves. Clip them together with wires so that they won't tumble.

*New Curtains and Bedspreads:*

1. Look at yard sales and thrift shops.
2. Consider buying bargain sheets. Make your own duvet (see Chapter 2) and your own curtains to match. They will be much cheaper than ready-made ones. It isn't hard, and most fabric stores give lessons.

*Wall Decorations:*

1. Check with your folks first. Ask how they feel about your putting up pictures with pushpins or some of the new picture-hanging gadgets or tapes. Hang a piece of your own artwork.
2. Go to a museum and buy prints from their gift shop.
3. Ask for a really nice picture or print for a birthday present. Go to a real art gallery and get the best print you can afford. Take extra good care of the print. Someday it may be valuable.
4. Get the art teacher to show you how to make a montage—a collection of pictures that are all pasted together to make one big picture. Cut them out of magazines, and paste them on an old bulletin board. When you finish, your picture will tell everyone who *you* are.
5. Start a photography hobby (it costs money!) and learn to mount and display your own work.
6. Buy shelves (get your folks' permission) and mount them high on the wall. Put them all the way around your room, and fill them with your collections.
7. Make a patchwork quilt of all your old worn-out clothes, and hang it on the wall. You can embroider something on each piece to help you remember when and where you wore it. Or write with liquid embroidery.

8. Call your local library and see if they rent or lend pictures.

*Desktop:*

1. Drugstores and variety stores like K-Mart and Woolworth's have many kinds of plastic desk accessories for not much money. You can also keep papers in stacking baskets for vegetables that you can buy at grocery and hardware stores. Buy on sale.
2. Get yourself a nonspill drinking mug—the kind with a wide flat bottom or the kind with a closed top. If you want to drink a cola or some milk while you do homework, it isn't as likely to spill as a glass or regular mug would be.
3. At yard sales pick up mugs or vases for a few pennies—a little crack in them won't hurt. Use them to hold your pens and pencils.
4. If you sometimes need a work space for your typewriter or sewing machine but don't have room for it, use a folding ironing board. Buy one at a yard sale. Check to see that it's sturdy. Stash it under your bed when you don't need it. The padding on it keeps the typewriter quiet and keeps it from slipping around.
5. Keep any food in your room in a plastic box with a tight-fitting cover or in a pretty tin. Don't encourage mice or ants or even your pet dog!

## Bathroom

*Storage and Decoration:*

1. Hang a plastic shoe bag on the shower rod to hold all the

shampoos, creams, etc. Each person in the family can have a different row.

2. Hang another shoe bag on the back of the door for everyone's dryers, curling irons, razors, etc.
3. Take advantage of the dampness of the bathroom and hang a plant on the wall that likes to be wet but doesn't need much light.
4. Hang a beach towel with a nice design to cover a stained wall.
5. If you share a bathtub with a baby brother or sister, hang a plastic mesh bag from the faucet or the shower rod to hold tub toys out of your way.


## School

1. Keep a supply of excuse blanks. You fill them out the day you return to school after an illness and get a parent to sign them.
   a. Make copies of the excuse blank on page 89 on a copy machine. Use carbon paper to keep a copy. Be sure to leave the carbon paper in until your parent signs. Keep the carbon copy at home so that you can prove your absences if school records get lost.
   b. Make excuse blanks on your computer. Use the computer to keep a record of your absences.
2. Buy a package of No Carbon Required (NCR is a trademark) paper at an office supply store. It's good for taking notes in school for a friend who is out sick. The friend can do the same for you when you're out sick.

## Family

*Getting Along:*

1. Ask your parents to set family rules and schedules. They can help solve problems like who uses the bathroom in the mornings and for how long and whose turn it is to do the dishes.

2. If you share a room with a Super Slob (or you are the Super Slob), use a curtain or a bookcase or a screen to divide the room. Then no one has to look at the other one's side.

*Emergencies:*

1. Organize and carry out a family fire drill. Decide how to get everyone out of the house, what everyone should do, and where everyone should meet.

2. Make a list of emergency and family phone numbers to be kept by each telephone. Use a pretty card or make a colorful poster. If it is going to be used by a little child, use photos or drawings to let them know what each number means.

## Celebrations

*Family Gifts:*

1. Use a camera to help your folks get organized and give them a gift at the same time. Go around the house and make photos of the furniture and appliances in every room. Put the date on the back of each picture. Give the pictures to your folks and tell them to put them away in a safety-deposit box or send them to a relative to keep. If there is a fire, storm, or burglary, the pictures prove to

the insurance company what was in the house. You can photograph cars or boats or campers for insurance, too.

2. While you have the camera, make photos of favorite toys of little brothers and sisters. Make or buy a small photo album for them. They'll love the pictures now and when they are grown.

*Planning Parties:*

Giving a party can be fun. But before you begin organizing a party, check out your party date and plans with your folks. If they agree, get busy!

If you've never given a party before, remember good old Secret #1. Break the problem down into small steps. Here are the steps we suggest:

1. List the people you'll invite. If you include most of the people in a special group of friends, invite everyone in the group. For example, don't invite eight of the people who run track with you and leave two out because you don't care for them as much. Hurt feelings can cast a cloud over the best party or over the next team meet.

2. Decide on a theme for the party. Parties that have a theme such as a fifties party or a Halloween costume party help you decide what to serve, what to do at the party, and how people should dress. At the end of this planning section, we'll give you some ideas for theme parties.

3. Plan (a) what you'll serve to eat and drink; (b) what decorations you'll use; and (c) what you'll do at the party (listen to music, dance, watch a video, play a murder mystery game). Think through the party. Picture your-

self when you begin to decorate and prepare refreshments and go through until cleanup after the last guest leaves.

4. As you think through the party, make a "To Do" list. If a special dish is needed, like a big platter for cold cuts, write down that you need to find one. If you plan to borrow special tapes or videos, put that down. If you're going to ask others to help with food, decorations, or music, list whom you'll ask and what you want them to do. As each person agrees, check that item off.

5. As soon as you decide what to serve, make a grocery list of what you need to buy. Include paper goods (throw-away plates, cups, napkins, tablecloth, and eating utensils) if you'll use them. Don't forget items like crepe-paper streamers, balloons, and favors, if needed. If you plan to take photos, add film, batteries, and flashbulbs to the list. Estimate how much everything will cost. If you go over your budget, decide what you can drop to stay within it.

6. Buy or make invitations. If you have a computer, design your own invitations. If not, and you want something different, buy a stamp pad and some rubber stamps. Gift shops and stationery stores have stamps in hundreds of designs, so you can probably find one with your party theme. Add the when, where, and what to wear (if needed), and your invitation's ready to go. Don't give them out at school. No one likes to know they are being left out of a party. It's best to mail the invitations or give them out after school.

7. Last-minute details always take longer than you think. Do as much as you can before the big day, such as shop-

ping and moving furniture and stereo equipment (check first with your folks).

*Party themes:*

1. *Pet Party.* With your folks' permission, celebrate your dog's or cat's birthday by inviting friends—with or without their pets. Be sure the pets can get along together if they come! As favors, give the pets a pet treat tied with a ribbon or yarn. For your human guests, bake cookies in the shape of animals or dog bones. Stores that sell baking supplies have these cookie cutters.

2. *Special Year Theme.* Your family or teachers can probably help you with this theme. Easy and popular years are the 1920's, 1950's, and 1960's. Look at yard sales for records and school yearbooks from the time period you pick. Ask at the library for books and magazines that show how those teens dressed. You may want to feature a special entertainer who was popular during that time. If you have a VCR, you can show a film from then.

3. *Beach Party.* The colder the weather, the more fun a beach party is! If you labeled your storage bags, you can easily find your shorts and swim clothes. Hang beach towels on the walls and use a raft or inner tube for decorations. Play records that remind people of summer. Cleanup is easy, since everyone sits on the floor on a sheet or beach towels and eats hot dogs or hamburgers off paper plates.

4. *Bingo!* A bingo party is a good choice when people of all ages get together for a block party or a family reunion. Ask everyone to bring something in good condition they no longer want. Display these items on a table so the winners can pick. Buy or rent bingo cards and markers.

Set up tables and have plenty of nibbles and drinks. Use squirt icing or cheese to decorate crackers, slices of cake, or toast like mini bingo cards.

5. *Chili Party.* Buy a large tub of chili and small sacks of corn chips at the grocery store. Split the chips bags open lengthwise and spoon the chili in. Eat with plastic spoons and play country-and-western or Cajun music.

6. *Super Subs Pot Luck.* Everyone brings a different thing to put on a sub. Buy a five-foot sub roll at a sub shop.

7. *Progressive VCR Party.* Start early in the afternoon at one house with popcorn and sodas, and watch a movie. Go

to the next house for dinner and another movie. Go to the last house for dessert and (oh dear) another movie.

*Want more ideas?* Skim through the catalogs that come to your house. Check through the teen magazines at the library. Be on the lookout for good ideas on TV. Start a collection of your own ideas.

If you find some organizing ideas or party ideas that work really well for you, send them to us at P.O. Box 335, Braddock Heights, Maryland 21714. We'll try to use them in another book.

Have a wonderful time!

# APPENDIX

Doodle Here

**RAP Sheet of** _____

Week of ___/___-___/

Subjects

**Monday**
Remember--

**Tuesday**
Remember--

**Wednesday**
Remember--

**Thursday**
Remember--

**Friday**
Remember--

Doodling space

Long-Term Assignments

Due
___/___
___/___

# Reports, Assignments, & Projects

RAP Sheet of _____

Week of ___/___/___

**Special To Do This Week**

- _____
- _____

| **Period** | **Homework for Monday** | **√ = Done** |
|---|---|---|
| _____ | _____ | _____ |
| _____ | _____ | _____ |
| _____ | _____ | _____ |
| _____ | _____ | _____ |
| _____ | _____ | _____ |

| **Period** | **Homework for Tuesday** | **√ = Done** |
|---|---|---|
| _____ | _____ | _____ |
| _____ | _____ | _____ |
| _____ | _____ | _____ |
| _____ | _____ | _____ |
| _____ | _____ | _____ |

| **Period** | **Homework for Wednesday** | **√ = Done** |
|---|---|---|
| _____ | _____ | _____ |
| _____ | _____ | _____ |
| _____ | _____ | _____ |
| _____ | _____ | _____ |
| _____ | _____ | _____ |

*Doodle here*

| **Period** | **Homework for Thursday** | **√ = Done** |
|---|---|---|
| _____ | _____ | _____ |
| _____ | _____ | _____ |
| _____ | _____ | _____ |
| _____ | _____ | _____ |
| _____ | _____ | _____ |

| **Period** | **Homework for Friday** | **√ = Done** |
|---|---|---|
| _____ | _____ | _____ |
| _____ | _____ | _____ |
| _____ | _____ | _____ |
| _____ | _____ | _____ |
| _____ | _____ | _____ |

| **B—I—G Reports & Projects** | Date Due |
|---|---|
| | / / |
| | / / |
| | / / |
| | / / |

**Remember . . .**
- _____
- _____
- _____
- _____
- _____

*Doodle Here*

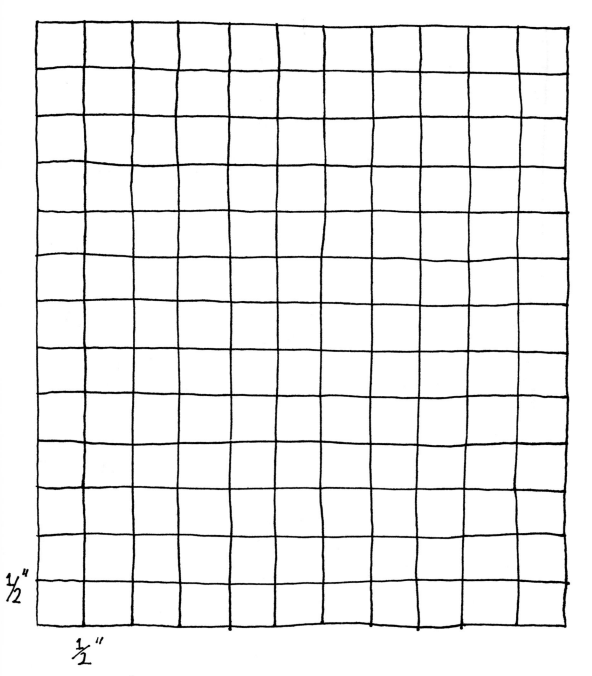

½"

½"

Scale: ½ inch = 1 foot

twin bed  twin bed

bedside tables

3 foot bookshelf

wastebasket

desk

floor lamp

bureau

desk chair

window

easy chair

doors

# EXCUSE SLIP

Please excuse _____
                        (full name)

on _____     _____
        (date, time)                        (Name)

was/will be  absent because _____
(cross out one)                    (reason)

_____

Thank you.

                              _____
                              (Signature of Parent/Guardian)

                                      ___/___/___
                                      (Date)